Hebrews

Leader Guide

DAVID A. deSILVA

HEBREWS
GRACE AND GRATITUDE

LEADER GUIDE

BY MIKE S. POTEET

Abingdon Press / Nashville

HEBREWS
GRACE AND GRATITUDE
LEADER GUIDE

Copyright © 2020 Abingdon Press

All rights reserved.

ISBN 13: 978-1-5018-9612-5

20 21 22 23 24 25 26 27 28 29—10 9 8 7 6 5 4 3 2 1
MANUFACTURED IN THE UNITED STATES OF AMERICA

Contents

Introduction 7

1. The Sermon's Setting and the Son's Glory
   (Hebrews 1:1–2:4) 11

2. Threshold Moments (Hebrews 2:5–4:13) 18

3. Responding Gracefully to Grace
   (Hebrews 4:14–6:20) 28

4. A Full, Perfect, and Sufficient Sacrifice
   (Hebrews 7:1–10:18) 37

5. Faithful Response in Action
   (Hebrews 10:19–11:40) 46

6. A Summons to Persevere in Gratitude
   (Hebrews 12:1–13:25) 56

Introduction

In *Hebrews: Grace and Gratitude*, Dr. David deSilva, Trustees' Distinguished Professor of New Testament and Greek at Ashland Theological Seminary in Ashland, Ohio, invites readers to read, reflect on, and respond to one of the New Testament's most rhetorically, theologically, and ethically challenging texts.

The Letter to the Hebrews is, as deSilva explains, actually a sermon in written form, addressed by a passionate Christian preacher to a congregation he feared was in danger of "drifting away" from the new life God had graciously made available to them in the death and exaltation of God's Son, Jesus. It is, as the author of Hebrews himself calls it, a "message of encouragement" (Hebrews 13:22) designed to motivate a first-century Christian community of faith to treat salvation as the precious gift it is: not a one-time transaction but an ongoing, dynamic relationship with God in which grateful response was not only proper but expected, in keeping with contemporary ethics of giving and receiving.

In his book's introduction, deSilva puts the core challenge of Hebrews to its audience, then *and* now, bluntly: "Does Jesus really offer you enough to make it worth investing . . . your whole life? . . . Do you ever wonder if perhaps God desires and deserves *more* from you, given what God has done and promises to do for you according to our faith?"

This Leader Guide will help facilitators guide small groups in reflecting on such serious and significant questions. Leaders and participants alike will get the most value out of the Guide by using it as they read Dr. deSilva's book; however, it may also be used as a companion to reading Hebrews itself. All scripture quotations in the Leader Guide, unless otherwise noted, are from the Common English Bible (CEB).

This Leader Guide contains discussion questions and occasional activities from which leaders may organize six sessions, corresponding to the six chapters in Dr. deSilva's book:

Session 1: The Sermon's Setting and the Son's Glory (Hebrews 1:1–2:4)

Participants will be introduced to the preacher's view of Jesus Christ and begin thinking about their life of faith as a series of investments in what God, through Christ, has already invested in them.

Session 2: Threshold Moments (Hebrews 2:5–4:13)

Participants will reflect on the significance of Jesus's solidarity with humanity and explore what perseverance in faith looks like in their own lives and situations and for Christians in other, more challenging contexts around the globe.

Session 3: Responding Gracefully to Grace (Hebrews 4:14–6:20)

Participants will examine the preacher's unique depiction of Jesus as a priest and will identify ways in which they, their community of faith, and other Christians respond to Jesus's priestly service with their own.

Session 4: A Full, Perfect, and Sufficient Sacrifice (Hebrews 7:1–10:18)

Participants will discover why the preacher of Hebrews connects the Old Testament figure of Melchizedek with Jesus and will recommit themselves to the priestlike service to which God calls all baptized believers.

Session 5: Faithful Response in Action (Hebrews 10:19–11:40)

Participants will ponder the meaning and consequences of "willful sin," and will also draw lessons for their own lives of faith from the great "cloud of witnesses" whom the preacher recalls in Hebrews 11.

Session 6: A Summons to Persevere in Gratitude (Hebrews 12:1–13:25)

Participants will consider the life of faith as a life of being trained and disciplined and will be challenged to commit to sacrificial ways of praising God and doing good.

Each session includes an opening and a closing prayer.

Group leaders will want to carefully read and reflect on each chapter of *Hebrews: Grace and Gratitude* before each session, in order to have a broader base of knowledge from which to answer questions; however, leaders are not expected to be experts in either Dr. deSilva's book or Hebrews itself and should feel free to say "I don't know" when appropriate, inviting participants to search for answers to questions together.

Group leaders will want to choose a comfortable meeting space physically accessible to all participants. Be sure to have Bibles on hand for participants who may not bring their own, at least one copy of *Hebrews: Grace and Gratitude*, and a copy of the accompanying DVD with a television or computer on which to play it. Leaders may want to have large sheets of paper or a marker board for writing down questions, answers, or notes from group discussion. Few sessions call for additional supplies, but they are listed when necessary.

May God use this study of *Hebrews: Grace and Gratitude* to inspire you and your group to grow in an appreciation of all we have been given in Jesus Christ and strength for responding more and more faithfully and gracefully!

A Note About Scripture Translation

In *Hebrews: Grace and Gratitude*, author David deSilva references his own translation of scripture from the Greek New Testament. This is a fantastic reminder of the first-century AD context in which the books of the New Testament were written, as well as the hard work of scholars and translators to make the Bible available to us in English today. DeSilva's translations also open the possibility for new insights into the meaning of a passage that might not be as apparent in many English translations.

In this Leader Guide, scripture quotations have been printed in the Common English Bible (CEB) translation. As you study the scripture passages each week, encourage your group to compare the CEB with deSilva's translations and note any differences and discuss what they might mean. You should also feel free to consult other translations. Comparing various Bible translations can often lead to a deeper understanding of a passage than reading a single translation can allow.

Session 1

The Sermon's Setting and the Son's Glory

(Hebrews 1:1–2:4)

Session Objectives

During this session, participants will:

- Reflect on experiences of giving and responding to gifts and connect these experiences to their Christian faith.
- Receive a broad overview of the content and original context of the Book of Hebrews.
- Read and discuss Hebrews 1:1-4 and 2:1-4 as foundations for Hebrews' overall message.
- Reflect on their investments in their Christian faith and how highly they value those investments.

Gathering

Welcome participants to this study of the Book of Hebrews and of *Hebrews: Grace and Gratitude* by David A. deSilva. Tell them about your interest in and enthusiasm for leading this study and ask them to share why they have chosen to participate.

Start a conversation about gifts participants have received and how they have responded to them. (Be ready to start discussion with your own answers to the questions.)

- What's the most memorable present you've ever been given, and what made it so?
- How did you respond to this present? Looking back, are you still satisfied with your response to the present? Why or why not?

- Have you ever given a present and been surprised or disappointed at the recipient's response? How, if at all, did the response and your reaction to it affect your relationship with the recipient?
- How are the relationships between human givers and recipients like or unlike God's relationship to us? Why?

Tell participants that, in *Hebrews: Grace and Gratitude*, David deSilva encourages us to read the Book of Hebrews as an extended discussion of what God has given God's people in Jesus Christ, and how God calls them to respond.

Read aloud from *Hebrews: Grace and Gratitude*: The author of Hebrews "dwells on the magnitude of God's gifts and of the place of unprecedented favor in which followers of Christ stand in order to magnify the importance of responding gratefully to such a Giver."

Opening Prayer

> Holy and faithful God, your generosity and grace are greater than we can conceive and deserve more gratitude than even our most profound thanks can convey. By your Spirit, guide us through this study to both a fuller awareness of all you have given us and a stronger commitment to responding in love and obedience every moment of our lives. This we boldly pray in the name of your Son, bringer of our salvation, Jesus Christ. Amen.

Skimming the Book of Hebrews

Invite participants to turn to Hebrews in their Bibles. Ask: "What do you already know or think about the Book of Hebrews?"

Ask participants to form small groups of two or three members. Have each group spend about five minutes skimming the whole Book of Hebrews, noting and discussing the main topics of the chapters and what seem to be important words, images, and ideas. Some Bible translations will have headings to guide the readers in this way; participants with study Bibles may have an outline or short overview of the whole book at the beginning of Hebrews to help their group.

After five minutes, have someone from each group share with the larger group about the team's findings. Write responses from each team on large pieces of paper or marker board.

Discuss:

- What words, images, and ideas show up the most in our quick overview of Hebrews as a whole?
- What did you notice the author having to say about what God has given to Christians?
- What did you notice the author having to say about how Christians should respond to God?

Video and Discussion

switch— Heb1:1-4

Watch Video 1 on the *Hebrews: Grace and Gratitude* DVD. After viewing, discuss the segment using some of the questions deSilva asks in the video. (Choose three or four that seem most interesting and relevant for your group.) They are repeated here for reference:

- How will I give Jesus and his gifts the attention and the investment that they merit? How will I bear adequate witness to Jesus and to his saving interventions in my life? What can I do with my life as a whole, what can I do in the specific situation or decision right before me, that will give Jesus the consideration, the service, the *gratitude* that he deserves?
- What do *you* think of Jesus?
- In what ways and to what extent are you giving the Son the attention that his dignity and his selfless generosity merit?
- What one or two changes might you need to make in your thinking and in your living to move further in that direction?
- What do you understand *deliverance—salvation*—to mean, and how important is it to you among the many pursuits that occupy your life?
- To what degree, and in what ways, does your life reflect a commitment to pay close attention to Jesus's announcement of deliverance?
- In what respects might the way you spend your time, energy, and resources suggest that you are yourself in danger of drifting?

You might also choose some of the questions below to go into deeper discussion of the video:

- Have you found "What would Jesus do?" a question that helps you live as a Christian? Why or why not? How would asking the *"am I thinking enough of Jesus?"*

question, "What does Jesus *deserve*?" shape your faith and action in different ways?

- Based on deSilva's discussion of the first-century context of Hebrews, how would you describe the book's author and its original audience? What connections can you make between their experience and your own?

- The preacher of Hebrews, says deSilva, believed those who have experienced God's favor in Christ only to disregard it are in a "more dangerous" place than those who have "never drawn near to God through Jesus in the first place." Do you agree? Why or why not?

- DeSilva says the preacher of Hebrews envisions "salvation" not so much as "something that happened for us when we first put our trust in Jesus" as "what will happen for us at the end of a lifetime of trusting and following Jesus." How do you react to this future-oriented view of salvation? How does it confirm or challenge the ways in which you tend to think about what salvation is and means?

- The author of Hebrews "is not at all reluctant to appeal both to the carrot and to the stick," deSilva observes. When, if ever, have you seen or experienced the power of "holy fear" to motivate greater faithfulness?

Reading and Discussing Hebrews 1:1-4

now video

In the past, God spoke through the prophets to our ancestors in many times and many ways. In these final days, though, he spoke to us through a Son. God made his Son the heir of everything and created the world through him. The Son is the light of God's glory and the imprint of God's being. He maintains everything with his powerful message. After he carried out the cleansing of people from their sins, he sat down at the right side of the highest majesty. And the Son became so much greater than the other messengers, such as angels, that he received a more important title than theirs.

After a volunteer reads the scripture aloud, use these or similar questions to discuss it:

- What specific words, phrases, or images grab your attention or your imagination as you hear the scripture? Why?

- As deSilva points out, Hebrews 1:1-4 is a single, artfully constructed sentence in the original Greek. How would you summarize the preacher's message in a single sentence of your own?
- What specific claims does the preacher make about who Jesus is and what Jesus does in this sentence? Why does each of these claims matter to the original audience? How much and why does each one matter to you?
- How is the preacher's depiction of Jesus in this sentence like and unlike the depiction of Wisdom found in Proverbs 8:22-34? Why does the preacher want to describe Jesus in ways that evoke older Jewish beliefs about God's Wisdom?
- The preacher focuses on the title "Son" for Jesus and continues to do so by quoting numerous "royal psalms"—those "that were composed with the Davidic king as their subject" (deSilva)—in 1:5-14. What does the preacher argue this title means? How is this understanding of Jesus as God's Son like or unlike your own? What other titles or images, if any, might communicate the preacher's understanding of Jesus as "Son" to a modern audience?
- The preacher claims that God spoke through Jesus in "these final days." What does this claim mean for readers living some two thousand years later? How much urgency do you feel about the way you respond to Jesus? Why?
- Why do you think the preacher begins addressing the community's crisis of faith and confidence in this way?

Reading and Discussing Hebrews 2:1-4

This is why it's necessary for us to pay more attention to what we have heard, or else we may drift away from it. If the message that was spoken by angels was reliable, and every offense and act of disobedience received an appropriate consequence, how will we escape if we ignore such a great salvation? It was first announced through the Lord, and then it was confirmed by those who heard him. God also vouched for their message with signs, amazing things, various miracles, and gifts from the Holy Spirit, which were handed out the way he wanted.

After a volunteer reads the scripture aloud, use these or similar questions to discuss it:

- These verses use a form of logical argument familiar from Jewish tradition: arguing from the lesser to the greater—"if this smaller thing is so, how much more must this bigger thing be so." (Jesus used this type of argument in, for example, Matthew 6:26-30.) Summarize the point of the preacher's "lesser to greater" argument in these verses. How convincing do you find it? Why?

- According to deSilva, "by the first century AD it had become commonplace to speak of angels having a role in bringing the Law from God to Moses." Does the preacher's argument in these verses diminish or enhance the Law's importance and value? Why? How important and valuable do you think the Law given to Moses is, and why?

- The preacher claims God's message through Jesus was confirmed by signs, miracles, and spiritual gifts. What stories from the New Testament would support this claim? Do you believe God confirms the message through Jesus in these ways today? Why or why not?

- Believers in the preacher's community who were "drifting away . . . were probably not thinking wrong things about Jesus," writes deSilva, "but they were certainly thinking *too little* of Jesus and of the deliverance and the salvation that he offered them." Which do you think is a more serious threat to believers today: thinking wrong things or thinking too little about Jesus? Which is a more serious threat to your own faith? Why?

Closing — *any questions to observations?*

Tell participants the two passages your group read and discussed in this session are foundations for Hebrews' overall message. Hebrews 1:1-4 stresses the gift God has given in Jesus; Hebrews 2:1-4 stresses the importance of grateful response to God's gift in Jesus.

Read aloud from *Hebrews: Grace and Gratitude*: "The preacher's audience had already made significant sacrifices in order to remain faithful to Jesus and to each other as long as they had. They needed assurance that they were making a good investment, that the reward would, in the end, justify the costs and the risks. They needed to know that they weren't just throwing away the only rewards of which human beings could be certain."

Ask participants to reflect silently on one or more of these questions:

- What, if anything, have you sacrificed to stay faithful to Jesus? To your faith community?
- How do you find assurance that your investments in your relationship to Jesus and your faith community are valuable?
- What more, if anything, do you believe God may be calling you to invest or sacrifice for your faith?

After allowing a few minutes for silent reflection, invite any volunteers to briefly share a response. Be prepared to share a response of your own.

Closing Prayer

Jesus Christ, Son of God, by your Spirit, help us pay ever greater attention to your message that we may not despise the great salvation you won for us when you made purification for our sins and took your place at the right hand of God. Amen.

Session 2

Threshold Moments

(Hebrews 2:5–4:13)

Session Objectives

During this session, participants will:

- Connect their experiences of unfinished literal journeys to the preacher's concern for his congregation's unfinished spiritual journey.
- Read about and reflect on the significance of Jesus's solidarity with humanity as described in Hebrews 2:5-18.
- Research the plight of Christians who face persecution around the world.
- Read and reflect on the preacher's call to perseverance in faith found in Hebrews 3:16–4:2, 11-13.
- Practice sharing their testimonies of faith with one another.
- Reflect on cultural and personal attitudes toward death in light of Hebrews' teaching about Jesus's death.

Gathering

Welcome participants to Session 2, especially any attending the study for the first time. Ask those who attended Session 1 to talk briefly about the key points they remember and how the session affected their faith and action.

Invite volunteers to talk briefly about trips they wanted to take but did not or trips they began but never completed. Ask (and be ready to begin discussion yourself if needed):

- What discouraged or prevented you from reaching your intended destination?

- What did you think and feel about not being able to take your trip or reach your destination?
- If you could take your untaken trip or finish your unfinished trip now, would (or will) you? Why?

Read aloud from *Hebrews: Grace and Gratitude*: "Jesus has pioneered for us the way to glory . . . [and] stands ever ready and willing to help us persevere in our own journey to ensure that we arrive at the goal. . . . The question remains, however: *Will* we persevere?" Tell participants your group will, in this session, explore ways the preacher of Hebrews encourages his audience to continue their journey of faith when they feel like giving up.

Opening Prayer

Compassionate and challenging God, you summon us to the journey of salvation. You invite and command us to follow your Son Jesus, who suffered in solidarity with humanity and whom you have now crowned with majesty. In this time of study, by your Spirit, may we receive your call more clearly and respond more readily, willing to risk what is passing away for the sake of the eternal glory you promise. Amen.

Video and Discussion

Watch Video 2 on the *Hebrews: Grace and Gratitude* DVD. After viewing, discuss the segment using some of the questions deSilva asks in the video. (Choose three or four that seem most interesting and relevant for your group.) They are repeated here for reference:

- What threshold moments have you encountered so far in your journey with God? How did God lead you—and perhaps carry you—to this point?
- What threshold moments do you face now, and what do you need from God to engage them faithfully?
- How real for you personally is the hope for life with God—indeed, a more immediate and intimate relationship with God—beyond death?
- Have you experienced the liberation from the fear of death of which the preacher is speaking?

- When has your hope of glory in God's presence helped you to make a difficult or costly choice for the sake of faithfulness to Jesus? How can this assurance help you make wise choices now with the challenges you currently face?
- How do you come to terms with passages of scripture that speak about God's anger toward the ungrateful and the disobedient?
- What role does the fear of God play in your own thinking and discipleship?
- What do our schedules, our allocations of our time and energies, suggest about our commitment to moving forward with God—and helping our sisters and brothers locally and globally keep moving forward with God?
- To what extent is your heart responsive to and to what extend is it hardened against the word that God speaks?
- Are there areas in your life where you don't welcome the intrusion of God's word?
- What would release you to be responsive to God's word even there?

Choose some of the questions below if you would like to go into deeper discussion of the video:

- In the video, deSilva mentions some threshold experiences— moments "when we're tempted not to go any farther . . . to turn back or at least to give up." What have been some significant threshold moments in your life? How did they turn out?
- What practical help for faithfully facing threshold moments does the preacher of Hebrews find for his congregation in Jesus's suffering and death?
- Do you think more often of death as "a threshold over which to cross," "a dead end to [your] journey," or something else? What experiences have shaped your attitude toward death?
- According to deSilva, "some churches stress" God's wrath "far too much and other churches, perhaps, far too little." How do we discern the difference between "too much" and "too little" emphasis on God's anger and its consequences? On which side of this divide do you think your church falls, and why? If your preachers and leaders started emphasizing God's wrath more or

less, how do you think the church would respond? What about your church's neighbors?

- "In our moments of greatest honesty with ourselves," says deSilva, "we might have to admit that we [like some ancient Israelites] are really more concerned with, and more invested in, securing our little piece of the world that is passing away than building our lives anew from the ground up on the foundation of Jesus's instructions." How strongly do you agree or disagree, and why?

Reading and Discussing Hebrews 2:5-18

God didn't put the world that is coming (the world we are talking about) under the angels' control. Instead, someone declared somewhere,

> What is humanity that you think about them?
>> Or what are the human beings that you care about them?
> For a while you made them lower than angels.
>> You crowned the human beings with glory and honor.
>> You put everything under their control.

When he puts everything under their control, he doesn't leave anything out of control. But right now, we don't see everything under their control yet. However, we do see the one who was made lower in order than the angels for a little while—it's Jesus! He's the one who is now crowned with glory and honor because of the suffering of his death. He suffered death so that he could taste death for everyone through God's grace.

It was appropriate for God, for whom and through whom everything exists, to use experiences of suffering to make perfect the pioneer of salvation. This salvation belongs to many sons and daughters whom he's leading to glory. This is because the one who makes people holy and the people who are being made holy all come from one source. That is why Jesus isn't ashamed to call them brothers and sisters when he says,

> I will publicly announce your name to my brothers and
> sisters.
>> I will praise you in the middle of the assembly.

He also says,

> I will rely on him.

And also,

> Here I am with the children whom God has given to me.

Therefore, since the children share in flesh and blood, he also shared the same things in the same way. He did this to destroy the one who holds the power over death—the devil—by dying. He set free those who were held in slavery their entire lives by their fear of death. Of course, he isn't trying to help angels, but rather he's helping Abraham's descendants. Therefore, he had to be made like his brothers and sisters in every way. This was so that he could become a merciful and faithful high priest in things relating to God, in order to wipe away the sins of the people. He's able to help those who are being tempted, since he himself experienced suffering when he was tempted.

After a volunteer reads the scripture aloud, discuss:

- The preacher quotes several passages from scripture (the Christian "Old Testament," but the only "testament" for the preacher and his congregation) in these verses. How is this preacher's use of scripture like or unlike modern preachers' use of scripture?
- Read Psalm 8. How would you summarize the psalm's content, tone, and message?
- As deSilva explains, the preacher finds the phrase "son of man" in Psalm 8:4 significant (also properly translated "human beings" in the CEB but obscuring the original Hebrew phrase). Why does the preacher want to make a connection between this phrase and Jesus's frequent name for himself, "the Son of Man" (CEB: "the Human One")? What point does the preacher want to make about Jesus, and why does he think his congregation should care? How much sense does the preacher's connection make to you? Why?

- "By showing [the congregation] Jesus," writes deSilva, "the preacher has shown them that the end of their story will also be honor and glory." What does the "honor and glory" God promises mean, specifically, to you? How much does the promise of it motivate you to live as Jesus's faithful follower?
- If someone were to ask you, "Why did Jesus have to die?" how would you respond? How does the preacher of Hebrews answer this question?
- In this passage, the preacher draws on verses from scripture to argue that Jesus claims us as his family—his "brothers and sisters" (verse 12), or his "children" (verse 13)—in order to argue that we must "live up to the confidence Jesus has in us" (deSilva). When have you believed that you failed to live up to Jesus's confidence in you? What about a time you believe you succeeded? How have these experiences shaped your faith and action since?
- The preacher's congregation faced disapproval and disavowal from their society because of their faith. What tests of your faith, what temptations to betray Jesus's confidence in you, do you face? How does knowing Jesus was tempted and tested affect the way you deal with your temptations?

Activity: Researching Believers Being Persecuted

Read aloud from *Hebrews: Grace and Gratitude*: "The fact that God did not shy away from [the congregation's] suffering but rather set it at the very center of God's own redemptive plan might challenge us also to bravely inquire into the plight of our sisters and brothers and apply ourselves fully to supporting them in the midst of their struggle to persevere in faith."

Ask participants to identify places where Christians today face persecution for their faith. Encourage participants with smartphones or other mobile devices to look for reputable online sources of information about Christian persecution today. (One such site is www.persecution.org/, the site of The Voice of the Martyrs, an international nonprofit defending Christians' human rights.) Ask:

- What does persecution of Christians look like in today's world?
- How would you respond to the claim, "Christians in the U.S. today are being persecuted"?

- What specific actions—as individuals, as our study group, as our congregation—do or could we take to support our persecuted sisters and brothers in faith?

Reading and Discussing Hebrews 3:16–4:2, 11-13

Who was it who rebelled when they heard his voice? Wasn't it all of those who were brought out of Egypt by Moses? And with whom was God angry for forty years? Wasn't it with the ones who sinned, whose bodies fell in the desert? And against whom did he swear that they would never enter his rest, if not against the ones who were disobedient? We see that they couldn't enter because of their lack of faith.

Therefore, since the promise that we can enter into rest is still open, let's be careful so that none of you will appear to miss it. We also had the good news preached to us, just as the Israelites did. However, the message they heard didn't help them because they weren't united in faith with the ones who listened to it. . . .

Therefore, let's make every effort to enter that rest so that no one will fall by following the same example of disobedience, because God's word is living, active, and sharper than any two-edged sword. It penetrates to the point that it separates the soul from the spirit and the joints from the marrow. It's able to judge the heart's thoughts and intentions. No creature is hidden from it, but rather everything is naked and exposed to the eyes of the one to whom we have to give an answer.

After a volunteer reads the scripture aloud, discuss:

- Read (or skim) Numbers 13:25–14:25. This story occurs after Moses has sent spies into Canaan, the land God promised to the Israelites freed from Egypt. How and why does Caleb and Joshua's report differ from the other spies' report about the Promised Land? How and why do the Israelites' and their leaders' (Moses and Aaron) responses to these reports differ? How and why does God respond to these events?
- According to the preacher of Hebrews, why did most of the Israelites in Numbers 13–14 fail to enter the Promised Land? What

connection does the preacher make between those Israelites and his congregation?

- Of the preacher's congregation, deSilva writes, "Each day the temptations and pressures they faced presented them with a threshold decision: Would they keep crossing over into God's future in faith, or would they look back longingly to the life and company they left behind?" When have you been tempted to look backward to something in your life that you have given up (or believe you should give up) in order to follow Jesus more faithfully? How do you deal with such temptations?
- The preacher, following Psalm 95, describes entering the future God promises as "entering God's rest." What does this description mean and suggest? How compelling a description of God's future do you find it, and why?
- "Far from trivializing our experiences in this life," writes deSilva, "the promise of entering God's rest magnifies the importance of how we choose to invest ourselves each and every day." What "investments" of time, energy, and resources are you making that will help you persevere in faith until you "enter God's rest"?
- The preacher describes God's Word as "living, active, and sharper than any two-edged sword." How does his own use of scripture in Hebrews illustrate and support his claim? When have you experienced the power of God through scripture to expose and judge your heart's thoughts and intentions?
- DeSilva believes the preacher would also count as God's Word "any means by which we might 'hear God's voice' speaking to us." What are some ways other than through scripture that you believe God has spoken to you?

Activity: Sharing Testimonies

The preacher of Hebrews urges those in his congregation to keep encouraging one another on their journeys toward God's rest (4:7). DeSilva writes, "When I hear a friend speak openly of how he or she has encountered God and experienced God's presence and movement in life, I am strengthened and confirmed in my own experience of God. Similarly, my sisters and brothers need the encouragement that comes from hearing how God has helped me in a given situation, how he has strengthened me to overcome

pause

this week

temptation, or how he has made his presence and direction known when I needed it."

Invite volunteers to share a testimony to God's presence and activity in their lives, perhaps in direct response to one of the situations deSilva describes. Provide paper and pencils or pens if participants would prefer to write their testimony. If you choose to use this activity, be ready to share a testimony of your own, especially if your group is not used to sharing personal testimonies.

If desired, discuss the activity using these questions:

- When have you been encouraged in your faith by the testimony of a fellow believer?
- When has your testimony encouraged someone else in their faith?
- "We deprive ourselves and one another of a great resource," deSilva writes, "when we believe the lie that faith or religion is a private matter." Do you agree that faith and religion are not private? Why or why not? What risks do we run in making our faith and religion public, and do you think the rewards of doing so outweigh the risks?

Closing

Read aloud from *Hebrews: Grace and Gratitude*: "How we look upon death holds great significance for how we spend our lives." Invite participants to think for a few minutes about the ways the culture in which they live views death. Ask them to name some specific examples of cultural attitudes toward death, as seen in popular media, familiar sayings, social customs, and so on. Ask: "When you think about death, what words, images, and feelings do you most often experience, and why?" Write notes on the discussion on the large paper or marker board.

Then read aloud from *Hebrews: Grace and Gratitude*: "Because Jesus unwaveringly walked the path of obedience to God knowing full well that it would lead to death—and, all the more, because God responded to Jesus's obedient death by raising him to a life that death could no longer touch—he showed us that death is not a dead end, but a threshold over which we pass on the way to glory. By doing so, Jesus broke death's mystical hold over our day-to-day lives." Ask:

- What practical difference does it or would it make for you, on a daily basis, to think about death as a final threshold instead of a dead end?

- How does or how could your congregation embody the truth that Jesus Christ breaks death's "mystical hold" over us?

Closing Prayer

Jesus, our brother, our Savior, we praise you for claiming us as your own; for becoming flesh of our flesh and bone of our bone; for presenting us to God in joy and confidence. May your Spirit make us worthy of the trust you place in us to follow where you lead and obey your commands, that we may experience your presence now and one day cross one last threshold into the peace of your rest, where we will glorify you and our God forever. Amen.

Session 3

Responding Gracefully to Grace

(Hebrews 4:14–6:20)

Session Objectives

During this session, participants will:

- Ponder connections between physical grace and spiritual grace by reflecting on images of "The Three Graces."
- Gain an understanding of dominant first-century attitudes toward gifts and gift-giving.
- Begin appreciating the preacher of Hebrews' depiction of Jesus as a priest by reading and discussing Hebrews 4:14–5:10.
- Wrestle with some of the preacher's difficult statements about his congregation's attitude toward grace by reading and discussing Hebrews 5:11–6:8.
- Identify specific examples of gracious responses to God's grace in the world, in their faith communities, and in their own lives.

Gathering

Before the session:

- Search online for images of the "Three Graces," which deSilva discusses in the video for session 3 of *Hebrews: Grace and Gratitude*. Choose several of these images to show your group. Try to select images that present the subject in different ways.
- Gather newspapers and magazines.

Welcome participants to Session 3, especially any attending the study for the first time. Ask those who attended Session 2 to talk briefly about the key points they remember and how the session affected their faith and action.

Show the group the images of the "Three Graces" you selected before the session. Don't explain the images at this point.

Ask participants:

- What do you think these images represent?
- Which one appeals to you most, and why? Which one appeals to you least, and why?

Now tell participants that (as deSilva will explain in today's video) these images represent the "Three Graces," three goddesses dancing together.

Ask:

- Do you enjoy dancing? If you do, what is your favorite kind of dancing? If you don't, why not? What memories of dancing, if any, do you have, and what do they make you think or feel now?
- Good dancers are often said to move gracefully. What connections can you make, if any, between physical grace and spiritual grace?

Tell participants this session explores how Christians can respond to God's grace in either grace*ful* or grace*less* ways.

Opening Prayer

Loving God, your Wisdom danced like a delighted child when you created the world, and in Jesus Christ, you have invited us to joyous celebration of life abundant and life eternal. As we again turn to scripture in dependence upon your Holy Spirit, may we discover how to follow faithfully the steps of your Son, learning and living his way of patient obedience and persistent love. Amen.

Video and Discussion

Watch Video 3 on the *Hebrews: Grace and Gratitude* DVD. After viewing, discuss the segment using the questions deSilva asks in the video. Choose three or four that seem most relevant and interesting to your group. They are printed here for reference.

- What does "maturing" in faith look like? What progress can you trace in your own growth in discipleship? What, if anything, do you find holding you back or distracting you from making progress?
- To what extent do you invest yourself in helping others grow in their faith and mature in their walk?
- In what ways have you experienced God's favor and assistance?
- To what extent have you shown God *and* the people around you that you value God's gifts and honor the Giver?
- How have you sought, and how do you continue to seek, to make a fruitful return to God and to Jesus for all the favor they have shown you?
- To what extent do your current investments of your time, talents, and resources show love for God by giving a range of support to fellow Christians in their journey to Christian maturity?
- When have you allowed yourself the level of openness before God in prayer that the preacher describes? What was the experience like, and what was the outcome? To what extent do you feel that God met you with what you needed to walk forward in faithfulness?
- What do you need to seek from the throne of grace in the present moment, to meet some challenge or cross some threshold that you currently face?

You may also wish to discuss the video further using the additional questions below:

- Do you tend to think of God's grace more as "a one-way transaction" or "a dynamic relationship," and why? How, if at all, has your thinking about God's grace changed over time?
- How would you answer the question asked of Methodist clergy, "Are you going on to perfection?" What evidence from your life would you point to in support of your answer?
- "The preacher [of Hebrews] sees no real middle ground between pressing on to maturity in Christ . . . and falling away" from him, says deSilva. Do you? Why or why not?
- DeSilva explains a first-century view of gift-giving: Gifts, or "graces," create long-lasting, reciprocal "relationships between people . . . committed to advance one another's interests in the world." How much, if at all, do you think this first-century

understanding of gifts and giving survives in modern society? How would more or less of the idea of gift-giving as a relationship, rather than a transaction, change society, and would that change be for the better or worse? Why?

- How accurately or appropriately do you think the image of the Three Graces deSilva shows and explains applies to the relationship between God and those to whom God gives the gift of salvation?

- DeSilva says the preacher wants his congregation to "look for ways to do God 'a good turn' whenever they can—which, in their case, means showing love and support for their fellow believers facing more significant hardship than they themselves do." What does "a good turn" for God look like in your case, or in your faith community's case?

Reading and Discussing Hebrews 4:14–5:10

Also, let's hold on to the confession since we have a great high priest who passed through the heavens, who is Jesus, God's Son; because we don't have a high priest who can't sympathize with our weaknesses but instead one who was tempted in every way that we are, except without sin.

Finally, let's draw near to the throne of favor with confidence so that we can receive mercy and find grace when we need help.

Every high priest is taken from the people and put in charge of things that relate to God for their sake, in order to offer gifts and sacrifices for sins. The high priest is able to deal gently with the ignorant and those who are misled since he himself is prone to weakness. Because of his weakness, he must offer sacrifices for his own sins as well as for the people. No one takes this honor for themselves but takes it only when they are called by God, just like Aaron.

In the same way Christ also didn't promote himself to become high priest. Instead, it was the one who said to him,

> *You are my Son.*
> *Today I have become your Father,*

as he also says in another place,

> *You are a priest forever,*
>   *according to the order of Melchizedek.*

During his days on earth, Christ offered prayers and requests with loud cries and tears as his sacrifices to the one who was able to save him from death. He was heard because of his godly devotion. Although he was a Son, he learned obedience from what he suffered. After he had been made perfect, he became the source of eternal salvation for everyone who obeys him. He was appointed by God to be a high priest according to the order of Melchizedek.

After one or more volunteers read the scripture aloud, discuss:

- "Priests played an important role in both Jewish and Greco-Roman religion," writes deSilva, "standing between human beings and God or the gods to build or repair bridges between the two, assure the favor of the divine toward the people, and secure for the people the assistance that only God or the gods could provide." How are priests, pastors, or other church leaders in your tradition like or unlike ancient priests? If your tradition does not include priests, is their mediating function played by others? How?
- The preacher of Hebrews starts "building a case" that Jesus—who was not, in his life on earth, a priest—is our "great high priest." What "qualifications" for Jesus's priesthood does the preacher point to in this section of his sermon? How do each of these qualifications represent an advantage for the preacher's congregation and for Christians today?
- How does the claim that Jesus was "tested" or "tempted" (both translations are accurate) "in every way that we are" (verse 15) but remained faithful shape the way you think about tests and temptations you have faced or are facing? To what extent do you believe Jesus's constant faithfulness to God is an achievable goal, and why?
- DeSilva notes that the preacher's reference to Jesus's "loud cries and tears" (verse 7) make "many readers . . . think about Jesus's prayer in the garden of Gethsemane," although the preacher may

instead have in mind the whole quality of Jesus's life, in which Jesus "had many occasions to wrestle with God in order to find the strength to commit to moving forward." How do you react to the idea that Jesus "wrestled with God" in an ongoing way? How frequently do you think of Jesus struggling to remain faithful to God's will? How would thinking of Jesus in this way more often shape your faith and your faithfulness?

- DeSilva proposes that, contrary to "standard translations," Hebrews 5:8 suggests "God heard (and answered) Jesus's prayers and pleas because of the reverent fear that Jesus exhibited; that is, God responded because of Jesus's virtuous disposition and not merely because" Jesus was God's Son. How do you react to this understanding? To what extent, if any, does it change how you think about the connection between human virtue and God's grace?

- "Jesus models how to pray with a view to persevering *through* suffering and difficulty," writes deSilva, "not with a view to escaping it." How much do your own prayers and your faith community's prayers follow Jesus's model in this regard? When, if ever, is it appropriate to pray to escape "suffering and difficulty"?

- According to deSilva, Jesus's life of prayer shows us prayer "does not need to be polite" but "to be honest. If we open ourselves up fully to God, God will encounter us in the depths of our being where we most need to find God's 'timely help.'" Would you describe your own prayers as mostly polite, mostly honest, or somewhere in between? Why?

Reading and Discussing Hebrews 5:11–6:8

We have a lot to say about this topic, and it's difficult to explain, because you have been lazy and you haven't been listening. Although you should have been teachers by now, you need someone to teach you an introduction to the basics about God's message. You have come to the place where you need milk instead of solid food. Everyone who lives on milk is not used to the word of righteousness, because they are babies. But solid food is for the mature, whose senses are trained by practice to distinguish between good and evil.

So let's press on to maturity, by moving on from the basics about Christ's word. Let's not lay a foundation of turning away from dead works, of faith in God, of teaching about ritual ways to wash with water, laying on of hands, the resurrection from the dead, and eternal judgment—all over again. We're going to press on, if God allows it.

Because it's impossible to restore people to changed hearts and lives who turn away once they have seen the light, tasted the heavenly gift, become partners with the Holy Spirit, and tasted God's good word and the powers of the coming age. They are crucifying God's Son all over again and exposing him to public shame. The ground receives a blessing from God when it drinks up the rain that regularly comes and falls on it and yields a useful crop for those people for whom it is being farmed. But if it produces thorns and thistles, it's useless and close to being cursed. It ends up being burned.

After a volunteer reads the scripture aloud, discuss:

- How do you react to the preacher's charge of spiritual laziness against the congregation? How would you respond if your preacher or spiritual leader leveled such a charge against your faith community?
- How does the preacher define spiritual maturity in these verses? How much or how little does it correspond with your own definition?
- What dangers, if any, exist in differentiating between less and more mature believers, and how does or could your faith community guard against those dangers?
- Why does the preacher use the metaphors of "milk" and "solid food" to distinguish different levels of instruction and growth in faith? What other metaphors can you think of that would also communicate the preacher's message?
- DeSilva describes Wesleyan class meetings as one way in which Christians could make progress toward holiness. When and how, if ever, have small groups helped you mature in your faith and practice? What small group opportunities for spiritual growth does or could your faith community offer?

- "We have many opportunities to take up our responsibility as Christians who are no longer 'infants' in the faith," deSilva writes. What are some opportunities you have taken advantage of as a maturing Christian to exercise responsibility in the faith community? What other opportunities to teach and lead other believers might God be calling you to consider?
- DeSilva suspects the preacher's comments about restoring wayward believers is "the most disputed passage in Hebrews." How does understanding of the dynamics of first-century gift-giving affect your understanding of this passage?
- DeSilva says the preacher of Hebrews, in addressing believers "before they have made the serious mistakes that he fears they might make," isn't addressing "penitent believers who have fallen away and wish to return to the community of faith." How does your tradition deal with such believers? What does your tradition teach about whether or not Christians can "lose salvation"? Do these teachings reflect Hebrews' understanding of salvation as the gift of a dynamic and continuing relationship with God? How?

Closing

Read aloud from *Hebrews: Grace and Gratitude*: "For [the preacher's congregation] now to withdraw, to walk away from the household of faith that God was drawing together, to confess to their neighbors (whether verbally or implicitly by their change in practice) that it was better to fit in and enjoy their good graces than continue to endure their hostility for the sake of some intangible homeland would mean bringing Jesus into further disrepute in the world instead of upholding his honor."

Distribute newspapers and magazines. Encourage participants to find news stories and articles they consider examples of Christians who are upholding Jesus's honor in the world today—graceful responses to God's grace—rather than "crucifying God's Son all over again and exposing him to public shame" (6:6). (You may also encourage participants who have smartphones or other internet-connected devices to look for examples from trusted sources.)

Ask:

- What is the most graceful response to God's grace you have ever personally seen or experienced?

- What is the most graceful response to God's grace you have seen your faith community make?
- What is one specific graceful response to God's grace you plan to make before our next session?

Closing Prayer

Grant us grace, O God, to serve you with grace, that by your Spirit the gifts you lavish on us may transform our relationships with one another, with our neighbors, and with you, so we may embody the freely given love you have shown in the life, suffering, death, and exaltation of your Son, our Savior, Jesus Christ. Amen.

Session 4

A Full, Perfect, and Sufficient Sacrifice

(Hebrews 7:1–10:18)

Session Objectives

During this session, participants will:

- Experience relying on a mediator and reflect on other experiences of mediation in their lives.
- Read and talk about the figure of Melchizedek in Genesis 14 and Psalm 110 and discuss why the preacher of Hebrews found him a significant character in understanding Jesus's priestly identity.
- Read and discuss the preacher's interpretation of Jeremiah's prophecy of a new covenant in Hebrews 8.
- Identify and commit themselves to ways in which they will obediently carry out priestlike service to God and others.

Gathering

Before the session, gather pieces of a construction toy such as LEGO bricks or a small quantity of quick-dry modeling compound, which you will use to assemble or sculpt a small object. You will need enough of the pieces or clay left over to make two copies of your object. For example, you might build a small structure out of LEGO bricks. Make your project simple enough to be completed in ten minutes or less but give it several distinct elements—parts of different sizes, colors, shapes, and so on. Be creative! (If you're feeling less than inspired, ask a child to build something for you; she or he may well be happy to do so!) Hide your finished structure or sculpture from view in your meeting space before participants arrive (behind a screen, for instance, or in an adjoining room).

You will also want to fill a large bowl with water and place it prominently in your meeting space (for use in the session closing).

Welcome participants to Session 4, especially any attending the study for the first time. Ask those who attended Session 3 to talk briefly about the key points they remember and how the session affected their faith and action.

Form two teams of participants and give each team the materials necessary to build a copy of your original and still-concealed project. Have each team to elect a "mediator." Show the mediators, but no one else, your original project. Give them one minute to look at and study it. Then send the mediators back to their teams, where they will guide the team in replicating the project. The mediators may only give verbal instructions and answer questions; they may not help build the duplicate projects themselves. After a predetermined amount of time (no longer than ten minutes), compare the teams' efforts to your original project.

Ask:

- What was this experience like for the mediator? for the team members?
- What made the mediators effective at helping their teams? What, if anything, would have made them more effective?
- How were the mediators in this activity like and unlike mediators in real life situations you've experienced or are familiar with?
- How is this activity a helpful or unhelpful illustration of how Jesus mediates our relationship with God?

Tell participants they will explore, in this session, the preacher of Hebrews' portrait of Jesus as our mediator. Read aloud from *Hebrews: Grace and Gratitude:* We "enjoy the great gift of being connected with a mediator—Jesus, the Son of God—who is in a better position to advance the relationship between God and human beings than any other mediator in history."

Opening Prayer

God Most High, who can possibly compare with you: enthroned in the heavens, yet looking upon us with enough favor to send your Son to make a new and living way for us into your presence? May your Spirit lift us into your company as we read and reflect on Holy

Scripture that we may grow ever more as your priestly people, mediating your truth and love to others as Jesus Christ, our great high priest, first mediates them to us. Amen.

Video and Discussion

Watch Video 4 on the *Hebrews: Grace and Gratitude* DVD. After viewing, discuss the segment using the questions deSilva asks in the video. They are printed below for reference.

- What has been your own experience of God's forgiveness, acceptance, even adoption into God's own family?
- How has this connection, if it is something you have experienced, impacted your orientation to and experience of life day-by-day?
- If "the blood of Christ . . . cleanses our conscience from dead works in order that we might serve a living God" (Hebrews 9:14), how do you think about discharging your own commission as a minister of the living God?
- How has he challenged his hearers thus far in his sermon to think about what is required of them, if they are to "continue" in this new covenant?
- What have you considered to be your part in regard to the new covenant, into which we are taken at our baptism, to which we commit ourselves in confirmation, and which we remember and celebrate whenever we receive communion?
- In what ways has the preacher stretched your understanding of your covenant obligations to God in Christ?

You may wish to discuss the video further using the questions below:

- Why were priests important in ancient religions, and why do they continue to be important in many religions today?
- As deSilva notes, the preacher of Hebrews uses "a kaleidoscopic assortment of Old Testament passages" to explain Jesus's identity and significance. Do you think the amount of time your community of faith, your preacher(s), and you spend personally reading, discussing, and reflecting on the Old Testament reflects its importance for knowing Jesus? Why or why not? If not, what changes could you suggest to others or make yourself?

- "And like the first covenant, so the new covenant must be put into effect by means of the shedding of blood." How comfortable are you thinking and talking about the blood of Christ in your own faith? Why? How does the image comfort or challenge you?
- "It seems," deSilva says, "the preacher of our sermon . . . laid great stock in the experience of knowing—and *feeling*—one's sins forgiven." When, if ever, was a time you knew and felt the forgiveness of your sins? How did you respond?

Reading and Discussing Hebrews 7:1-25

This Melchizedek, who was king of Salem and priest of the Most High God, met Abraham as he returned from the defeat of the kings, and Melchizedek blessed him. Abraham gave a tenth of everything to him. His name means first "king of righteousness," and then "king of Salem," that is, "king of peace." He is without father or mother or any family. He has no beginning or end of life, but he's like God's Son and remains a priest for all time.

See how great Melchizedek was! Abraham, the father of the people, gave him a tenth of everything he captured. The descendants of Levi who receive the office of priest have a commandment under the Law to collect a tenth of everything from the people who are their brothers and sisters, though they also are descended from Abraham. But Melchizedek, who isn't related to them, received a tenth of everything from Abraham and blessed the one who had received the promises. Without question, the less important person is blessed by the more important person. In addition, in one case a tenth is received by people who die, and in the other case, the tenth is received by someone who continues to live, according to the record. It could be said that Levi, who received a tenth, paid a tenth through Abraham because he was still in his ancestor's body when Abraham paid the tenth to Melchizedek.

So if perfection came through the levitical office of priest (for the people received the Law under the priests), why was there still a need to speak about raising up another priest according to the order of Melchizedek rather than one according to the order of Aaron? When the order of the priest changes, there has to be a change in the Law as well. The person we are talking about belongs to another tribe, and no one ever served at the altar from that tribe. It's clear that our Lord came from the tribe of Judah, but Moses never said anything about priests from that tribe. And it's even clearer if another priest appears who is like Melchizedek. He has become a priest by the power of a life that can't be destroyed, rather than a legal requirement about physical descent. This is confirmed:

> You are a priest forever,
>> according to the order of Melchizedek.

On the one hand, an earlier command is set aside because it was weak and useless (because the Law made nothing perfect). On the other hand, a better hope is introduced, through which we draw near to God. And this was not done without a solemn pledge! The others have become priests without a solemn pledge, but this priest was affirmed with a solemn pledge by the one who said,

> The Lord has made a solemn pledge
> and will not change his mind:
> You are a priest forever.

As a result, Jesus has become the guarantee of a better covenant. The others who became priests are numerous because death prevented them from continuing to serve. In contrast, he holds the office of priest permanently because he continues to serve forever. This is why he can completely save those who are approaching God through him, because he always lives to speak with God for them.

After one or more volunteers read the scripture aloud, discuss using these or similar questions:

- Have participants turn to Genesis 14. Tell them that, at this point in Genesis, Abraham—who has responded to God's call to become father to a great, chosen people by traveling to the land God has promised him (Genesis 12:1-4)—has rescued his nephew Lot from local kings, including the king of Sodom. Have a volunteer read aloud Genesis 14:17-24. Point out that this passage is Melchizedek's only appearance in the Torah. What do we know about him from it? What does he do?

- Have participants turn to and read Psalm 110, which contains the only other mention of Melchizedek in the Old Testament. Who is Psalm 110 about, and why does the psalm-singer mention Melchizedek?

- What claims does the preacher make about Melchizedek? Why is each of these claims important to what the preacher says about Jesus?

- "It stuck in Israel's memory," writes deSilva, "that there was at one time a priest of the One God who was not descended from Levi," as Israel's priests were, "but rather predated [Levi's] birth." Why is this "memory" of priests outside the system of priesthood inherited by descent from Levi important to the preacher's identification of Jesus (who "came from the tribe of Judah," verse 14) as not only a priest but a better priest?

- Why does the preacher so urgently claim Jesus "can completely save those who are approaching God through him" (verse 25)? What would the consequences be if Jesus were not completely able to do so? Why would they matter to the preacher and his congregation? Why might they matter to you and your faith community?

- How effectively do you think the image of a priest communicates the preacher's point about Jesus as "a better mediator, a better go-between connecting human beings and God" in today's world? What other images, if any, might communicate this message as well or even more powerfully, and why?

Reading and Discussing Hebrews 8:1-13

Now the main point of what we are saying is this: We have this kind of high priest. He sat down at the right side of the throne of the majesty in the heavens. He's serving as a priest in the holy place, which is the true meeting tent that God, not any human being, set up. Every high priest is appointed to offer gifts and sacrifices. So it's necessary for this high priest also to have something to offer. If he was located on earth, he wouldn't be a priest because there are already others who offer gifts based on the Law. They serve in a place that is a copy and shadow of the heavenly meeting tent. This is indicated when Moses was warned by God when he was about to set up the meeting tent: *See that you follow the pattern that I showed you on the mountain in every detail.* But now, Jesus has received a superior priestly service just as he arranged a better covenant that is enacted with better promises.

If the first covenant had been without fault, it wouldn't have made sense to expect a second. But God did find fault with them, since he says,

Look, the days are coming, says the Lord,
when I will make a covenant with the house of Israel,
and I will make a new covenant with the house of
Judah.

It will not be like the covenant that I made with their ancestors
on the day I took them by the hand to lead them out of
the land of Egypt,
because they did not continue to keep my covenant,
and I lost interest in them, says the Lord.

This is the covenant that I will make with the house of Israel
after those days, says the Lord.
I will place my laws in their minds,
and write them on their hearts.
I will be their God,
and they will be my people.
And each person won't ever teach a neighbor
or their brother or sister, saying, "Know the Lord,"
because they will all know me,
from the least important of them to the most important;
because I will be lenient toward their unjust actions,
and I won't remember their sins anymore.

When it says new, it makes the first obsolete. And if something is old and outdated, it's close to disappearing.

After one or more volunteers read the scripture aloud, discuss using these or similar questions:

43

- According to the preacher, in what ways does Jesus's presence with God in heaven make Jesus a better priest than those who serve on earth?
- Many religions viewed (and still view) their worship spaces as copies or reflections of heavenly spaces, or at least as sacred space in some way. The Israelites' tabernacle in the wilderness (and later the temple in Jerusalem) was believed to mirror God's heavenly court. To what degree does the idea of sacred space influence how your faith community treats where it worships? How can such an attitude benefit the community? How can it become a burden?
- How does the preacher quote Jeremiah 31:31-34 to define the "better promises" (verse 6) God makes through Jesus?
- Read or skim Jeremiah 31. In their historic context (the time of the Jewish people's exile in Babylon, some five to six centuries before Jesus), what do the verses the preacher quotes anticipate? How do you imagine Jeremiah's original audience, or devout Jews in the first century, would have responded to the preacher's interpretation of these verses?
- DeSilva summarizes the preacher's argument: "Jesus's ministry is more excellent [than the ministry Levitical priests perform] because it is more effective" in securing forgiveness of sin and ongoing access to God, and so the preacher identifies "God's new arrangements with the Christian community as a better covenant, the new covenant." What risks does the church run in proclaiming the preacher's message today, after past and continuing anti-Semitism, often committed in the name of Christianity? How, if at all, can the modern church talk of a "better covenant" without claiming Judaism is "old and outdated" or "close to disappearing" (verse 13)?

Closing

Standing or sitting near the large bowl of water you prepared before the session, read aloud Hebrews 10:22: "Therefore, let's draw near with a genuine heart with the certainty that our faith gives us, since our hearts are sprinkled clean from an evil conscience and our bodies are washed with pure water." Explain that the preacher of Hebrews is likely referring to baptism, the ritual of initiation into the Christian community.

Read aloud from *Hebrews: Grace and Gratitude*: The preacher "speaks of Jesus having made his followers 'clean' specifically 'to go about serving the living God' . . . This is the language of priestly service." Though, as deSilva notes, the preacher does not call the congregation "priests," he does expect them to "continually offer up a sacrifice of praise through" Christ, and "to do good and to share what [they] have, because God is pleased with these kinds of sacrifices" (Hebrews 13:15-16).

Encourage silent prayer and reflection on what "sacrifices of praise" God is calling participants to offer. Invite volunteers to come and sprinkle themselves with water from the bowl, as a reminder of their having been consecrated to God's priestlike service in their baptisms.

Closing Prayer

> In grace, O God, you claim us for your service. Send us out now in the strength of your Spirit, not only to proclaim your glory with our lips but also and especially to embody it in our lives, for that is the role you have prepared for us: obeying you as did your Son, our Savior, Jesus Christ. Amen.

▷ It's a sermon (≈ 70-90 AD)

▷ inviting us to think highly + think always of Jesus

▷ so we will hold fast to faith even in hard times when the cost seems high

▷ God is developing God's relationship w/ us, even tho we have failed in the past — we have a new & permanent high priest — a renewed covenant written within (in addition to w/out) ▷ we are looking forward to completion!

Session 5

Faithful Response in Action

(Hebrews 10:19–11:40)

Session Objectives

During this session, participants will:

- Consider how they can make specific investments of themselves in God's freely given gifts.
- Reflect on the preacher's teachings about "willful sin" and its consequences in Hebrews 10:23-36.
- Explore the "heroes of faith" in Hebrews 11, why the preacher chose to highlight them for his congregation, and how these individuals remain relevant to participants' faith communities.
- Commit to at least one specific way of seeking approval by God's standards rather than those of the surrounding culture.

Gathering

summarize briefly

Welcome participants to Session 5, especially any attending the study for the first time. Ask those who attended Session 4 to talk briefly about the key points they *so far* remember and how the session affected their faith and action.

observe Ask participants to identify, by name, some people whose pictures they have displayed in their home or collected in photograph albums or photo books. Encourage them to talk briefly about why these people are important to them.

Explain that during this session they will be studying Hebrews 11, which could be considered a kind of "photo album" of faith or a great display of "family photos." But read aloud this reminder from *Hebrews: Grace and*

46

Gratitude: "The so-called faith chapter . . . is not something that is easily lifted from its context in the sermon or the immediate context the preacher was addressing." In this session, the group will explore why.

Opening Prayer

> *Eternal God, in every age you have called people to live by hope: hope in your presence, your power, and your promises. As we attend once more to the preacher of Hebrews, may we discover in his ancient words your fresh and always living words of challenge and encouragement that we may grow as faithful followers of Jesus Christ. Amen.*

Video and Discussion

Watch Video 5 on the *Hebrews: Grace and Gratitude* DVD. After viewing, discuss the segment using the questions deSilva asks in the video. Choose the three or four that seem most relevant and interesting to your group. They are printed below for reference.

- In what ways are you seeking to "draw closer" to God and to the goal of the journey we began at baptism (in terms of moving toward both maturity in discipleship and our eternal homeland)?
- To what extent and in what ways are you holding onto the *profession* of our hope in Christ, both internally and in your outward witness?
- How have you been attentive to the preacher's call to look closely *at* and look *after* your sisters and brothers in the family of God, both locally and globally, encouraging their perseverance through your love and acts of support?
- What role do concern for God's honor and, more especially, fear in regard to affronting God play in your own decision-making processes?
- When has your sense of being accountable before God and facing the consequences of faithless choices led you in a direction that proved healthful to your discipleship and life?
- Has the fear of God or an image of God that overcompensates in the direction of God's anger ever played a hurtful role in your walk of faith?

- Where have similar considerations as those that guided these heroes of faith been at work to give your present life the shape that it currently has?

- What impact would it have on the shape of your life today and in the days ahead were you to give greater weight to the invisible, the future, and the life beyond death that drove these exemplary figures?

- What figures loom large for you in the cloud of witnesses that you carry about in your mind and heart? What do they teach you about faithful living and how has this impacted your life?

- What is the visible testimony to God and God's promises that can be read by others in your life? What effects in how you live your life give evidence to others of the divine Cause that has acted upon you?

You may wish to discuss the video in more depth using the questions below to prompt further conversation.

- When have you most recently put "yourself out to help another person get access to what he or she needed"? How did the person respond? What did you think and feel because of the experience?

- "The preacher urges his hearers . . . to gladden the heart of God" by matching the Son's commitment and investment in them with theirs to him. What committed investments does your faith community make that you believe gladden God's heart?

- DeSilva says "willful sin," for the preacher of Hebrews, is "deciding that God's gifts are not worth the cost of keeping them." What costs of keeping God's freely given gifts can you think of? When, if ever, have you been tempted to try to avoid such costs? What happened?

- How would you describe "faith" to someone unfamiliar with the concept? How much is your definition like or unlike the preacher's as deSilva describes it in this video?

- "The cloud of witnesses has, of course, expanded exponentially in the more than nineteen centuries since the preacher drafted his own dream line-up." Whom would you add to the "line-up" of faithful heroes? Why?

Reading and Discussing Hebrews 10:23-36

Let's hold on to the confession of our hope without wavering, because the one who made the promises is reliable.

And let us consider each other carefully for the purpose of sparking love and good deeds. Don't stop meeting together with other believers, which some people have gotten into the habit of doing. Instead, encourage each other, especially as you see the day drawing near.

forward looking

If we make the decision to sin after we receive the knowledge of the truth, there isn't a sacrifice for sins left any longer. There's only a scary expectation of judgment and of a burning fire that's going to devour God's opponents. When someone rejected the Law from Moses, they were put to death without mercy on the basis of the testimony of two or three witnesses. How much worse punishment do you think is deserved by the person who walks all over God's Son, who acts as if the blood of the covenant that made us holy is just ordinary blood, and who insults the Spirit of grace? We know the one who said,

fallen away

> Judgment is mine; I will pay people back.

And he also said,

> The Lord will judge his people.

It's scary to fall into the hands of the living God!

(we should be more concerned about pleasing God than placating enemies)

But remember the earlier days, after you saw the light. You stood your ground while you were suffering from an enormous amount of pressure. Sometimes you were exposed to insults and abuse in public. Other times you became partners with those who were treated that way. You even showed sympathy toward people in prison and accepted the confiscation of your possessions with joy, since you knew that you had better and lasting possessions. So don't throw away your confidence—it brings a great reward. You need to endure so that you can receive the promises after you do God's will.

ongoing zeal (clues about dangers ahead)

After one or more volunteers read the passage aloud, discuss using these or similar questions:

- According to deSilva, the "confession" (CEB) or "profession" (NRSV) of hope in verse 23 can mean both "internal assent or agreement" about the Gospel and "public affirmation" of it. How does your faith community balance internal agreement with public affirmation? Which aspect of confession does it find easiest, and why? How could it grow in the other?

- How have members of the preacher's congregation invested "*themselves* in showing greater love and lending support" (deSilva) as a result of considering "each other carefully" (verse 24; see verses 32-34)? When have you decided to invest yourself more heavily in your fellow believers because you paid more attention to them? How did these investments affect your faith?

- DeSilva asks, "If we were to look intently" at our persecuted sisters and brothers in faith elsewhere in the world, "how might we be stimulated to respond with love and good works" for them? How will you make careful consideration of Christians in parts of the world where the church faces greater challenges a more regular part of your own spiritual practice?

- Explain in your own words the comparison and contrast the preacher draws between disobeying the Law God gave to Moses and rejecting the truth God reveals in Jesus. What do you think about the point the preacher wants to make?

- "Given the situation his Christian hearers were facing," writes deSilva, "the preacher no doubt thought of 'willful sin' . . . as drawing back from the Christian community." How serious do you consider withdrawing from the faith community to be? Under what circumstances, if any, might drawing back be a faithful path rather than a faithless "path of least resistance"? How do Christians who might want to withdraw from the community balance their perspective and motivations against how their withdrawal might publicly affect "God's honor and the honor of the Son"?

- Commenting on the preacher's description of God's wrath, deSilva writes, "Many of us shy away from the notion as perhaps too primitive a view of God, yet our scriptural heritage promotes this understanding consistently." How do you react to the idea of the "fear of God"? How prevalent is this idea in your faith community as a whole? How can fear of "the consequences of abusing God's honor" help us more accurately and consistently value God's grace? In your judgment, does a focus on the fear of God do more harm or good? Why?

Reading and Discussing Hebrews 11:1-2, 8-19, 23-40

Faith is the reality of what we hope for, the proof of what we don't see. The elders in the past were approved because they showed faith.

[Abraham and Sarah]
By faith Abraham obeyed when he was called to go out to a place that he was going to receive as an inheritance. He went out without knowing where he was going.

By faith he lived in the land he had been promised as a stranger. He lived in tents along with Isaac and Jacob, who were coheirs of the same promise. He was looking forward to a city that has foundations, whose architect and builder is God.

By faith even Sarah received the ability to have a child, though she herself was barren and past the age for having children, because she believed that the one who promised was faithful. So descendants were born from one man (and he was as good as dead). They were many as the number of the stars in the sky and as countless as the grains of sand on the seashore. All these people died in faith without receiving the promises, but they saw the promises from a distance and welcomed them. They confessed that they were strangers and immigrants on earth. People who say this kind of thing make it clear that they are looking for a homeland. If they had been thinking about the country that they had left, they would have had the opportunity to return to it. But at this point in time, they are longing for a better country, that is, a heavenly one. Therefore, God isn't ashamed to be called their God—he has prepared a city for them.

By faith Abraham offered Isaac when he was tested. The one who received the promises was offering his only son. He had been told concerning him, *Your legitimate descendants will come from Isaac.* He figured that God could even raise him from the dead. So in a way he did receive him back from the dead. . . .

[Moses and the Israelites]
By faith Moses was hidden by his parents for three months when he was born, because they saw that the child was beautiful and they weren't afraid of the king's orders.

By faith Moses refused to be called the son of Pharaoh's daughter when he was grown up. He chose to be mistreated with God's people instead of having the temporary pleasures of sin. He thought that the abuses he suffered for Christ were more valuable than the treasures of Egypt, since he was looking forward to the reward.

By faith he left Egypt without being afraid of the king's anger. He kept on going as if he could see what is invisible.

By faith he kept the Passover and the sprinkling of blood, in order that the destroyer could not touch their firstborn children.

By faith they crossed the Red Sea as if they were on dry land, but when the Egyptians tried it, they were drowned.

By faith Jericho's walls fell after the people marched around them for seven days.

By faith Rahab the prostitute wasn't killed with the disobedient because she welcomed the spies in peace.

[Conclusion]
What more can I say? I would run out of time if I told you about Gideon, Barak, Samson, Jephthah, David, Samuel, and the prophets. Through faith they conquered kingdoms, brought about justice, realized promises, shut the mouths of lions, put out raging fires, escaped from the edge of the sword, found strength in weakness, were mighty in war, and routed foreign armies. Women received back their dead by resurrection. Others were tortured and refused to be released so they could gain a better resurrection.

But others experienced public shame by being taunted and whipped; they were even put in chains and in prison. They were stoned to death, they were cut in two, and they died by being murdered with swords. They went around wearing the skins of sheep and goats, needy, oppressed, and mistreated. The world didn't deserve them. They wandered around in deserts, mountains, caves, and holes in the ground.

All these people didn't receive what was promised, though they were given approval for their faith. God provided something better for us so they wouldn't be made perfect without us.

[handwritten margin note: we must endure a hard past]

Invite participants to skim Hebrews 11, the "so-called faith chapter," in its entirety. Ask volunteers to share short reactions—a single word or brief phrase, without further comment at this point—to the chapter once they have skimmed it.

Read aloud verses 1-2 and discuss:

- In the original Greek text, as deSilva explains, the preacher defines faith (*pistis*) as the *hypostasis* (high-PAW-stuh-siss)—the "foundation," origin, strategy for construction, or "deposit"—"of what we hope for," and the *elenchos* (eh-LENG-kuss)—a "legal term meaning 'evidence' or 'proof' "—"of what we don't see." How does knowing something about the original words shape your understanding of the preacher's definition? How is it like or unlike the way you usually think about "faith"?
- DeSilva also explains that modern translations can accurately render these verses as more subjective ("what our experience of trusting *feels* like") or as more objective (faith "essentially puts the things for which we hope in our possession, . . . and gives 'proof' to the world of the invisible realities that move us"). How important are both of these dimensions to a full understanding of faith? Do you tend to think about faith more subjectively or objectively? Why?
- Given what you have discovered through this study of Hebrews about the temptations facing the preacher's congregation, why do you think the preacher wants to define faith for them in this way?

[handwritten margin note: unfaith we live on the assumption God's promises be true]

Form three groups of participants and assign each group a section of Hebrews 11 to read and discuss more closely, following the divisions supplied in this guide: "Abraham and Sarah" (verses 8-19), "Moses and the Israelites" (verses 23-31), and the conclusion (verses 32-40). Ask each group to consider these questions in its conversations:

- How, specifically, do the people in these verses demonstrate faith?
- Why do you think the preacher chose to showcase these particular examples of faith for his congregation?
- How relevant are these specific examples of faith to your congregation, and why?

After allowing sufficient time for discussion, invite a volunteer from each small group to briefly discuss highlights of the group's conversation with everyone.

You may wish to provide these questions to the groups, or use them to guide a discussion with the full group:

- *"Faith acts with a view to the unseen,"* writes deSilva, and so defies "the widespread perception that only what can be experienced by the five senses is 'real.'" Where do you encounter this perception in society and culture today? How, specifically, do the people in Hebrews 11 challenge such a "materialist" perspective? How, specifically, does your faith lead you and your congregation to challenge this perspective?
- "Walking by faith," writes deSilva, "requires taking God's announcements about the future with utmost seriousness." How do the people in Hebrews 11 demonstrate that seriousness about God's promised future? What promises from God about the future do you take most seriously, and why? Which ones are you tempted to doubt, and why? How does what we believe about or expect to happen in the future shape the way we live today?
- DeSilva notes that *"faith invests in eternal goods."* What eternal investments do the people in Hebrews 11 make? How is your congregation, and how are you personally, investing tangibly and practically in "eternal goods"? Which prevalent social values do such investments challenge, and how?
- DeSilva also points out *"faith acts in the confident hope of the Resurrection."* Bible scholars generally agree resurrection was a late theological development in Judaism, and the Old Testament figures

the preacher mention lived long before Jesus. How did they, in the preacher's judgment, nonetheless have hope in the resurrection? How does faith in the resurrection free people of faith from fear of and intimidation by opposition? How does your faith community express hope in the resurrection?

Closing

Read aloud from *Hebrews: Grace and Gratitude*: "The preacher challenges all Christians to decide for whose approval they will live. If we look for God's approval in everything we do, asking what will lead God to say, 'Well done,' we will enjoy the peace of single-mindedness and integrity of life."

Distribute pieces of scrap paper or index cards. Read this list of areas in which deSilva asks readers to consider what would merit God's approval. Invite participants to write down one specific way they will seek to follow God's standards rather than cultural standards in at least one of these areas. Pause to allow silent reflection and time for writing after each item on the list:

- Making decisions
- Facing temptations
- Choosing employment
- Lifestyle and spending habits
- Use of time

Encourage participants to look over their lists and set an intention to fulfill these commitments to God.

Closing Prayer

Jesus Christ, our strong Savior, we rely on your Spirit to strengthen us as we strive to live faithfully. Inspired by those who have gone before us and focused on your victory for us, may we increasingly live as those who have been created for eternity and communion with the invisible God, your Father and ours. Amen.

Session 6

A Summons to Persevere in Gratitude

(Hebrews 12:1–13:25)

Session Objectives

During this session, participants will:

- Connect experiences of physical training and discipline with their experiences of growth in faith and commitment to God.
- Reflect on ways members of the community of faith help (or can help) one another endure in faithful living.
- Commit to specific, practical, and sacrificial ways of praising God and doing good.

Gathering

Welcome participants to Session 6. Ask those who attended Session 5 to talk briefly about the key points they remember and how the session affected their faith and action. Also ask participants if they have remaining questions or observations related to the study as a whole that they want to be sure to address in this session; incorporate these suggestions into your group's discussion to the extent you can.

Ask participants to talk about any athletic figures (famous or not) whom they admire. Ask:

- What have these athletes achieved that participants find praiseworthy? What training or discipline have these athletes undergone to realize these achievements?
- Have you undergone rigorous training and/or discipline? What was the experience like?

56

Tell participants that this session considers the ways God trains and disciplines us to live as faithful witnesses to Jesus.

Opening Prayer

Faithful God, as we end our study of Hebrews today, may we remember our responsibility and privilege to live as your glad and grateful followers and witnesses, which will not end until we come, at last, to the city you have prepared for us. May your Spirit use this time to nourish our commitment to you that we may more fully answer the commitment you have shown and continue to show us in Christ, the pioneer and perfecter of faith. Amen.

Video and Discussion

Watch Video 6 on the *Hebrews: Grace and Gratitude* DVD. After viewing, discuss the segment, using the questions deSilva asks in the video. Choose three or four that seem especially relevant or interesting for your group. They are printed here for reference:

- What weight might God be calling *you* to set aside in order to run well in the direction of living more and more fully for Jesus, of yielding more completely to him the life he ransomed at the cost of his own?
- How can you help one another, as brothers and sisters in Christ, to shed these particular weights, as well as any sinful entanglements?
- What stumbling blocks stand in the way of extending genuinely the love of sisters and brothers to one another within your congregation? How can you help level those stumbling blocks?
- How can you and the other members of your group grow in the virtue of hospitality and in the good fruits in the lives of others it can produce?
- In what ways and to what degree are we attentive to the global family of faith, whose perseverance in faith could be facilitated by our expressions of love, hospitality, and practical support?
- In what ways have you been and are you being summoned to "go out" from the structures our society has built for us and our lives, seeking out new ways of forging community around God and God's values and vision?

- In what ways are your weekly practices and activities shaped by what is "normal" or "typical" for people brought up in our culture, and in what ways are they shaped by what God has prescribed through his Son, his prophets, and his apostles to occupy God's people?

You may wish to discuss the video further using the questions below to prompt additional conversation:

- DeSilva describes some of the realities the preacher's congregation would have faced that might have drawn their attention from Jesus. What realities "get the lion's share of [your] attention in any given moment" that threaten to (or sometimes do) distract you from Jesus? What do you do to refocus your attention? How does or how could your faith community help?
- The preacher of Hebrews emphasizes the members of the faith community's "mutual responsibility to watch out for one another," says deSilva, "to intervene in one another's lives in ways that help each other . . . stay on track with God." When have you seen such intervention take place in your faith community? How easy or difficult do you find initiating such intervention, and why? How, if ever, have you benefited from your fellow believers' intervention?
- "Our family in Christ is the treasure we take with us when we die," says deSilva. How does taking this statement with utmost seriousness transform a faith community's life together now?

Reading and Discussing Hebrews 12:1-17

So then, with endurance, let's also run the race that is laid out in front of us, since we have such a great cloud of witnesses surrounding us. Let's throw off any extra baggage, get rid of the sin that trips us up, and fix our eyes on Jesus, faith's pioneer and perfecter. He endured the cross, ignoring the shame, for the sake of the joy that was laid out in front of him, and sat down at the right side of God's throne.

Think about the one who endured such opposition from sinners so that you won't be discouraged and you won't give up. In your struggle against sin, you haven't resisted yet to the point of shedding blood, and you have forgotten the encouragement that addresses you as sons and daughters:

My child, don't make light of the Lord's discipline
or give up when you are corrected by him,
because the Lord disciplines whomever he loves,
and he punishes every son or daughter whom he
accepts.

Bear hardship for the sake of discipline. God is treating you like sons and daughters! What child isn't disciplined by his or her father? But if you don't experience discipline, which happens to all children, then you are illegitimate and not real sons and daughters. What's more, we had human parents who disciplined us, and we respected them for it. How much more should we submit to the Father of spirits and live? Our human parents disciplined us for a little while, as it seemed best to them, but God does it for our benefit so that we can share his holiness. No discipline is fun while it lasts, but it seems painful at the time. Later, however, it yields the peaceful fruit of righteousness for those who have been trained by it.

So strengthen your drooping hands and weak knees! Make straight paths for your feet so that if any part is lame, it will be healed rather than injured more seriously. Pursue the goal of peace along with everyone—and holiness as well, because no one will see the Lord without it. Make sure that no one misses out on God's grace. Make sure that no root of bitterness grows up that might cause trouble and pollute many people. Make sure that no one becomes sexually immoral or ungodly like Esau. He sold his inheritance as the oldest son for one meal. You know that afterward, when he wanted to inherit the blessing, he was rejected because he couldn't find a way to change his heart and life, though he looked for it with tears.

After one or more volunteers read the passage aloud, discuss using these or similar questions:

- Why does the preacher frame the life of faith as an athletic contest in these verses (as deSilva notes, a race in verse 1 and a wrestling match in verse 4)? To what other athletic contests, if any, would you compare your experience of striving to live faithfully? What other instances of, in deSilva's words, "hardship as the path to enjoying an honorable victory" might function as good analogies for the life of faith, and why?

- How and why does the "great cloud of witnesses" (verse 1) encourage the preacher's congregation in this extended athletic metaphor? How, if at all, do you find encouragement to live faithfully from those who have lived faithfully before you?

- How did Jesus show himself to be the greatest example of faith as the preacher defined faith in Hebrews 11? What's the significance of calling Jesus, as deSilva notes the original Greek text does, "the 'perfecter of faith'—not 'the perfecter of our faith' . . . but of 'faith' itself"?

- DeSilva writes, "Considering how much Jesus endured on [the congregation's] behalf . . . should both embolden and shame them to endure as much for Jesus in return." How effectively does shame motivate people to faithful living, in your judgment? How, if at all, is the preacher's use of shame different from "shaming people into" something? To what extent do you think it appropriate to compare our efforts at faithfulness with Jesus's efforts? Why?

- "The preacher understood," writes deSilva, "and wanted his hearers to understand, that Jesus's death for them did more than transfer some gift to them. It bound the parties together in a life-debt, with those who have received Jesus's benefits bound to give back to Jesus." How do you respond to the "life-debt" image as a description of your relationship to Jesus? Do you think it is a relevant and meaningful metaphor for today's society? Why or why not?

- DeSilva says the preacher thinks the difficulties his congregation face are "a sign of God's favor" that proves "their divine adoption." How do you respond to the preacher's assertion? What is the difference between viewing "discipline" as divine punishment for wrongdoing (a view deSilva says the preacher doesn't share) and as "God testing, training, and shaping the wise person through hardships, making him or her worthy of God's company"? How could (or how has) this distinction helped you or your faith community consider hardships you've faced in a different way?

- What other ways of speaking about learning obedience to God, if any, could or should the church use?

- DeSilva suggests the preacher's view of discipline "speaks, once again, very directly to Christians in repressive nations." How much does the social context in which the church lives affect how it hears these teachings about discipline and obedience? Do you think the preacher's teaching encourages Christians in nonrepressive contexts to do more or less for their fellow believers elsewhere? Why?

- The preacher invokes the story of Esau to warn his congregation. Read Esau's story in Genesis 25:29-34 and 27:30-40. What do you think of the preacher's use of Esau "to drive home the foolishness of jeopardizing eternal benefits for temporary pleasure" (deSilva)? Do you think the preacher accurately and fairly characterizes Esau? How does Esau's behavior in Genesis 33:1-4 affect your view of him? How do you imagine Esau would react to hearing the preacher's sermon?

- When, if ever, have you been tempted to choose "temporary pleasure" over "eternal benefits"? How did you handle the temptation? How would you advise fellow Christians facing similar temptations?

Reading and Discussing Hebrews 13:1-14

Keep loving each other like family. Don't neglect to open up your homes to guests, because by doing this some have been hosts to angels without knowing it. Remember prisoners as if you were in prison with them, and people who are mistreated as if you were in their place. Marriage must be honored in every respect, with no cheating on the relationship, because God will judge the sexually immoral person and the person who commits adultery. Your way of life should be free from the love of money, and you should be content with what you have. After all, he has said, *I will never leave you or abandon you.* This is why we can confidently say,

> The Lord is my helper,
>   and I won't be afraid.
> What can people do to me?

Remember your leaders who spoke God's word to you. Imitate their faith as you consider the way their lives turned out. Jesus Christ is the same yesterday, today, and forever!

Don't be misled by the many strange teachings out there. It's a good thing for the heart to be strengthened by grace rather than by food. Food doesn't help those who live in this context. We have an altar, and those who serve as priests in the meeting tent don't have the right to eat from it. The blood of the animals is carried into the holy of holies by the high priest as an offering for sin, and their bodies are burned outside the camp. And so Jesus also suffered outside the city gate to make the people holy with his own blood.

So now, let's go to him outside the camp, bearing his shame. We don't have a permanent city here, but rather we are looking for the city that is still to come.

After one or more volunteers read the passage aloud, discuss using these or similar questions:

- As deSilva explains, the preacher calls his hearers to love one another with *philadelphia* (verse 1): the ideal loving relationship of "trust, solidarity, and cooperation," reciprocal sharing, mutual protection, and harmony between siblings. When have you experienced philadelphia within a faith community? What practical steps can a faith community take to encourage the flourishing of philadelphia?
- Why was hospitality a critical element of the early church's life? In what specific ways does your faith community practice hospitality, especially to those whom the rest of your society often marginalizes? Have you ever been "hosts to angels without knowing it" (verse 2)?
- How does your faith community remember and minister to prisoners (verse 3)?
- How does your faith community support those who are married in honoring their marital commitments (verse 4)? How do you show support to those members who, by circumstance or choice, are not married?
- "'Contentment,'" deSilva writes, "is not a core value in capitalist economies." In what specific ways does your faith community encourage believers to free themselves from the love of money, as the preacher urges (verse 5)?
- What does it mean to you to proclaim Jesus Christ as "the same yesterday, today, and forever" (verse 8)? When, if ever, has

this promise proved especially meaningful to you? How do we distinguish between Jesus's unchanging nature and changing understandings of Jesus, and when is it important to do so?

- What is the "altar" to which the preacher refers in verse 10, and why does he contrast it with the sacrificial worship system of Israel? How does this contrast connect with the preacher's presentation, earlier in Hebrews, of Jesus as a high priest?

- Why does the preacher emphasize Jesus's death "outside the city gate" (verse 12)? What are the risks of being "outside" society—either physically or outside society's norms and expectations? How does your faith community accept these risks in service to Jesus? How have you personally experienced the risk of being "outside" as a result of your discipleship?

Closing

Read aloud Hebrews 13:15-16:

> So let's continually offer up a sacrifice of praise through him, which is the fruit from our lips that confess his name. Don't forget to do good and to share what you have because God is pleased with these kinds of sacrifices.

Tell participants that deSilva explains how praising God "would indeed be a 'sacrifice' for the preacher's audience, since the quieter they were about their connection with Jesus, the better things would go for them, but such was the 'thank offering' that Jesus, their mediator, and God, their heavenly benefactor, merited."

Ask participants to think about one specific way they could praise God and "do good" (verse 16) that would feel like or actually be a "sacrifice" for them. Invite volunteers to share with the group (and, of course, be ready to begin discussion by sharing your own response aloud). Ask participants to commit to praying for one another during the next week, that they will carry through on their plans for sacrificial praise and good works.

Before reading the closing prayer together, thank participants for attending and contributing to this study of Hebrews. Invite volunteers to offer any final thoughts or comments on Hebrews, on deSilva's book, or on the study experience as a whole.

Closing Prayer

Read Hebrews 13:20-21 aloud in unison:

May the God of peace,
> who brought back the great shepherd of the sheep,
> our Lord Jesus,
> from the dead by the blood of the eternal covenant,

equip you with every good thing to do his will,
> by developing in us what pleases him through Jesus
> Christ.

To him be the glory forever and always. Amen.